COLLECTED POEMS
MARY BARNARD

COLLECTED POEMS

MARY BARNARD

BREITENBUSH PUBLICATIONS

PORTLAND, OREGON

Also by Mary Barnard
Sappho: A New Translation
The Mythmakers

Copyright © 1979 by Mary Barnard.
Introduction copyright © 1979 by William Stafford.
First printing August 1979.
First paperback printing October 1981.

Library of Congress Cataloging in Publication Data
Barnard, Mary, 1909-
    Collected Poems
    I. Title
(79-54693)
ISBN (paper) 0-932576-09-5

Breitenbush Books are published for James Anderson
by Breitenbush Publications.
Mailing address P.O. Box 02137, Portland, Oregon 97202.
Printed in the USA by Press-22, Portland, Oregon.

To Rex Arragon, humanist,
and to his wife, Gertrude,
who, as Tibor Serly said,
is *no slouch*, herself!

Acknowledgments

Some of these poems were previously published in a collection entitled *Cool Country*, which formed one section of the New Directions anthology, *Five Young American Poets, 1940*. Others were collected in *A Few Poems*, 1952.

Most of the poems collected here were first published (sometimes under a different title or in a slightly different version) in the following periodicals: *Poetry* (Chicago), *Partisan Review*, *Furioso*, *Tiger's Eye*, *New English Weekly* (London), *Townsman* (London), *Westminster Magazine*, *New Letters*, *Encore*, *Odysseus*, *Agenda* (London), *New Democracy*, *Harper's Bazaar*, *Providence Journal*, *Saturday Review of Literature*, *Origin* (Kyoto), *Woman Poet*, *The New Republic*, and *New Directions in Prose and Poetry*, 1936 and 1937. "The Pleiades" was first published in *The New Yorker*. "Later" has also appeared as a set of four postcards published by the Prescott Street Press.

Mary Barnard's Poems: An Introduction

It is strange that this book hasn't happened before. Mary Barnard published her first poem, outside school publication, in 1935—"Shoreline," included here. And throughout the '30's and on into the present her work has flourished.

But her poetry has never been brought together, except for small gatherings (a section in *Five Young American Poets*, by New Directions in 1940, and in *A Few Poems*, 1952). For someone so accomplished, this lag in the collecting is remarkable—and some of the reasons are instructive. Even as early as 1933 Mary Barnard was in touch with Ezra Pound, and he coached her and approved her work ("Lethe," in this collection, was in the first group of poems he considered from her). He liked the idea that she was studying Greek, and he thought she "had an ear;" besides, he responded sympathetically to "the shattering wail of the segregated and lone poet on the far, far coast."

That reaching out, from Pound, was encouraging, but the far, far coast did isolate, in those days. True, the area provided background for poems (Mary Barnard's father managed a sawmill at Buxton, and associations of that kind loom in poems like "Roots," "Cool Country," "The Axe," "Logging Trestle," "Highway Bridge," "Planks," "The Orchard Spring," "Noon Hour" . . .); but the Northwest was far different from the background shared by most flourishing poets of the '30's. Mary Barnard's ability did take her into that group on occasion. She had two summers at Yaddo, in upstate New York, during the decade, and there she met people like Muriel Rukeyser, Kenneth Fearing, Eleanor Clark, Henry Roth, Babette Deutsch, Malcolm Cowley, Reuel Denney, and Delmore Schwartz. Much less political than these, Mary Barnard felt herself something of an outsider, and continued to follow her own course.

And we must remind ourselves that there was the Depression. Travel was difficult, and money—especially for foreign travel—was not there for Mary Barnard till much later. From 1939 to 1943 she was Curator of the Poetry Collection at the University of Buffalo. This was a rich time for reading and writing and encountering authors; but by the time she left Buffalo she felt a surfeit of poetry, and turned to prose. She did historical research for Carl Van Doren in the following years, and published short stories in *The Yale Review*, *The Kenyon Review*, and *Harper's Bazaar*.

It was later, in 1951, during an illness, that Mary Barnard harked back to her studies in Greek, and from that into her well-known translation of Sappho. That translating enticed her back into poetry. Her prose, however, continued to be important; and dissatisfaction with "the authorities" in her research for the Sappho project led her to ten years of work that eventuated in *The Mythmakers* (1966).

These apparent excursions from her own poems simply broadened the base for her writing. From the work on Sappho would come such elements as the "fragments" included in "Later." Her reading for *The Mythmakers* brought forth such poems as "The Pleiades," "A Picture of the Moon," and "E.P. Martinsbrunn." By now her background could span from the Pacific experience ("Shoreline," "Ondine," "Storm," "Wine Ship") to the international literary company indicated above.

Mary Barnard's way of doing a poem had begun with a grammar school fascination with jingles, rhymes, and ballads. Even in college she was writing in conventional meters, with end-rhyme. (And she still likes the idea of conventional verse in school, with plenty of chance to explore the pleasures of sound.)

In her third year at Reed College, she studied creative writing under Lloyd Reynolds, who persuaded her to loosen up; and she began to learn that free verse need not mean Carl Sandburg or Edgar Lee Masters or Amy Lowell—all of whose work lacked appeal—but could mean Pound and H.D. and T.S. Eliot.

From that background came these poems. There is the part from traveling back roads of Washington and Oregon with her father, buying lumber from small mills. There is the tuning and the immersion in the classics—even early, during the study at Reed, and later with associates like Pound. There is the example, for literature and for life, in the work of William Carlos Williams and Marianne Moore. And there are the involvements with such enrichments as the Poetry Library at Buffalo and the research for translations and myths.

Strange, that this book hasn't happened before. Now it has happened; readers can have the whole span of this distinctive work, with its scholarship, its enrichment from current literary life, and its never-relinquished perspective of being alone—somewhat—on the far, far coast.

WILLIAM STAFFORD
Lake Oswego, Oregon
1979

Contents

Playroom

Wheel of sorrow, centerless.
Voices, sad without cause,
slope upward, expiring on grave summits.
Mournfulness of muddy playgrounds,
raw smell of rubbers and wrapped lunches
when little girls stand in a circle singing
of windows and of lovers.

Hearing them, no one could tell
why they sing sadly, but there is in their voices
the pathos of all handed-down garments
hanging loosely on small bodies.

The Fitting

She is imprisoned among mirrors
while a trio of hags with the cold hands
of elderly dressmakers entangle,
bind and define her body with tape-measures.
They compress withered lips upon pins.

Again and again she will re-enact
this fitting. Censure will be a knuckle
shocking the flushed skin; all women
these women, their muttered words
breathing distortion upon the mirror's reflection.

The knocking of hammers comes
from beyond the still window curtain
but her hands will make nothing:
her life is confined here, in this depth,
in the well of the mirrors, on the carpet
the pulled threads, at her heel the scissors
making a soft snipping sound.

The Tears of Princesses

The tears of princesses were cool as rain.
They wept purely into their unbound hair.
Tears were ornaments to be hung
at the pale eyelid like jewels
at the coral lobe of the ear.

Princesses had long beautiful names
and they always cried with perfect reasonableness
for lasting sorrow or bloody-hilted
abhorrent wickedness
presented at the unguarded breast.

Princesses melted, sugar-and-dew, in privacy,
in dungeons, towers, or lying on forest moss;
but never, never were their eyes scalded with hot salt,
their chins dripping, their mouths swollen
just anywhere, for nothing, for no reason
but having too many tears.

The Orchard Spring

Not in the forest with its air of childhood—
the secret fern, the tree tops
run through with wind—
but in an orchard planted and grown
in the traditions of men,
I heard for the first time
an ancient sequence of words, a rhyme
that like the fragrance of warm grass
tempted an illusive appetite
but seemed meaningless.

A doorsill was buried in the dew
of a steep orchard: from what quarter
did the difference come
to unsettle that room?
A twelfth-century nightingale
half-heard, still, in the western coast range
of the continent, troubles
the dreams of little green children.

Doves, gold rings, words
out of the English island.
Fresh delight of rain on our hillsides
and the earth answering with springs.

Seedlings

The plum thicket is
a dark green covert
sheltering the ricked up

fireplace lengths
of alder that blew
down in the storm.

Sprouting underfoot
like spring beauties
are desires for one

day's worth of childhood.
I could make a play-
house here with stones.

Shoreline

The sea has made a wall for its defence
of falling water. Those whose impertinence
leads them to its moving ledges
it rejects. Those who surrender
it will with the next wave drag under.

Sand is the beginning and the end
of our dominion.

The way to the dunes is easy.
The shelving sand is stiffened in the rain
and loosened again in the sun's fingers.
Children, lustful of the glistening hours,
drink and are insatiate. Wind under the eyelids,
confusion walling the ears, their bodies glow
in the cold wash of the beach.
                                        And after,
they walk with rigid feet the planked street of the town.
They miss the slipping texture of the sand
and a sand pillow under the hollow instep.
They are unmoved by fears
that breed in darkening kitchens at sundown
following storm, and they rebel
against cold waiting in the wind and rain
for the late sail.

                    Did you, as I,
condemn the coastal fog and long for islands
seen from a sail's shadow?
                                    The dunes lie
more passive to the wind than water is.
This, then, the country of our choice.

It is infertile, narrow, prone
under a dome of choral sound:
water breaking upon water.

Litter of bare logs in the drift—
the sea has had its sharp word with them.
Wild roses, wild strawberries cover the dune shoulder.
It is a naked restless garden that descends
from the crouched pine
to shellfish caught in flat reflecting sands.

We lose the childish avarice of horizons. The sea ends
against another shore. The cracked ribs of a wreck
project from the washed beach.
Under the shell-encrusted timbers
dripping brine
plucks at the silence of slant chambers
opening seaward. What moving keel remembers
such things as here are buried under sand?

The transitory ponds and smooth bar slide
easily under the advancing tide,
emerging with the moon's
turning.
            Clear lagoons
behind the shattered hulk, thin
movements of sea grass on the dune rim
bending against cloud, these things are ours.
Submissive to the sea and wind,
resistful of all else, sand
is the beginning and the end
of our dominion.

Cool Country

This green is the pod,
the enveloping color of our triangular valleys
where rivers still young spring
from the coast range into salt estuaries.

Mist blown between promontories
saturates the earth's every crevice,
making the grass deep and sweet in all seasons
and the forest heavy.

From these come the red cheeses,
the apricot-colored lumber, deckloads
moving into the green like lanterns.
The pod is broken for vermilion steaks of the salmon,
the chill wave itself opened
for the red-ripeness of harvest.

Roots

Rain on the windshield,
roads spongy with sawdust
have meant in the end
a love of place that grows into the body.
Blood should be clear amber under tree bark.

Lacking that, there are the roads
extending like root tendrils
under the angles of mountains,
rain sharpening on the windshield at evening.

The Axe

The axe lies in shadow at the house-root,
hoarding its sharpness, menacing
as a nervous fang. Pause to search it out
while the eyes drink in darkness, then step
carefully away from it into chips
by the frayed block, remembering:

how when the old lady drew off her gloves I saw,
in spite of myself, the three finger-stumps,
the sight cloaking me with a sickness.

Sheer off, back of the chimney. Creep
over the wheelbarrow; keep clear of it.
If ever I have not enough kindling,
and the fire dies, I shall
have to go cold.

But the woodcutter praises God for his fine days
in heavily-barked ricks by the wood-road.
The two tracks bright with chips
meander through fern. His axe is the laughter
made where hill warps against hill.
The swing of the axe-head in its arc
has threaded his shoulders.
Ha! and the sound is tossed back, hill
to hill. Steel strikes a deep wound—
Ha! and the bearded lips of the hills
are cracked with laughter—O, it's the merry axe-blade.

Carry, you with the weak wrists, your ten
long cold fingers tucked in a shawl
up basement stairs. Hark! It's the merry axe-blade!

Beds

Sleep, to the chirruping incantations of night, rises
like vapor in lowland pastures, clouding the eyes of children.
Lulla, lulla, will there be, will there
always be a place to sleep when smoke gathers under the rafters?

The carved oak headboards of ancestral beds tilt
like foundered decks from fog at the mouth of the river.
Lulla, lulla. Flood after flood. When the beds float
downstream, will there be a place to sleep, Matthew, Mark?

Will new beds be sold in those aisles where soft-eyed brides
are shopping with gift money for the bed of Odysseus?
Instead of the rooted olive, sham walnut, a bed in the wall,
a mattress on the shed floor. Will there be this?

The damp webs, answering, tangled against my face at nightfall
in the pink festival of fireweed and on pumice beaches.
The feathers of my grandmothers' beds melted into earlier darkness
as, bone to earth, I lay down. A trail that leads out, leads back.
Leads back, anyway, one night or another, bone to earth.
Bat wings traced the water and sleep was pure.

II

The Rapids

No country is so gracious to us
as that which kept its contours while we forgot them,
and whose valleys, closed under receding hills,
open to our return.

The water we saw broken upon the rapids
has dragged silt through marshland
and mingled with the embittered streams of the sea.
One might have kept sweet pailsful and kept nothing.

But the ungatherable blossoms floating by the same rock,
the chisel marks on a surface in full flight
have flung light in my face, have made promises
in unceasing undertone.

Logging Trestle

Neither cloud nor rain casts
a chill into the valley
like that of a trestle fallen into disuse.

The rails move out from the hillside
across the piling lengthening its stroke
where ground slopes riverward.

Abruptly, the rails terminate.
Sky opens between the cross-ties lifted
each upon five upright timbers. The gray wood

leads the eye to nothing further.
The broken column stands against cloud
as though an abandoned wharf extended into wind.

Highway Bridge

When a hill stream enters a river at flood
it is abashed into stillness, welling
between grass blades and small clover.
Its surface becomes the green of leaves obstructing light,
tranquil between piers.

Although the bridge has a purpose other
than the quiet under it, a peace
exploded by the rapid wheels overhead,
after their passage this that we thought shattered
absorbs the falling fragments of sound.
There is a deeper silence than before
where two ruts dip under the river's border
and do not reappear.

Planks

Footsteps upon fine gravel drop into silence
like pebbles into water at close intervals.
Circles of air break on the dark mountains.

Strange how hard it is to balance
in the pit of the evening, distances
spreading upward, making the head light.
But walking feet have their own pleasure,
touching rhythmically the hard earth.

Dry planks lying under the bank attract them.
The moment is completed neither
by fragrance of wild lilac, nor by
the presence of the darkening river,
but by the feel of wood underfoot
and the sound of stepping upon thick planks.

The River Under Different Lights

1. The Gorge

Light has the dull luster of pewter
and the clouds move sidewise clawing the tops of the crags,
resting their soft gray bellies
briefly in high valleys.

Foam, plowing against the rapids
gathers all brightness.

2. The Ship

A ship that passes inland between mountains
moves as though resting from the sea's labor.

Riders in the fogging buses peer
at snatches of river between madrona and fir,
at the prow of a white vessel
dividing reflected forests:
a gesture compact with stillness.

3. The Estuary

Where fresh water meets salt
a single wave shears
the fog with a slow edge
lifted by tide or current or
hull's pressure.

Nothing is sure, neither
tide, season, nor hour
in this flux of stream and ocean,
daylight and fog,
where only the fish,
a secret presence, move
surely on spring's errand.

Storm

A vessel is breaking in half under the headland.
The ocean is swollen with storm and the lives
of the drowned men. Foam drawn over them.

Above my left eye a pain burrows.
Conspirator, awaiting dangerous weather,
if I were there, you would be suffocation,
pain and the ocean obliterating each other.

The radio brings Bach from Philadelphia.
Closer within than sickness and outside death
the well-plumed music drives beyond the lighthouses
towards the extreme coastland—
    ἀκτὰν πρὸς ἑσπέρου θεοῦ
                            On our beaches
dead sea birds under yellow curds of foam.

Journey

Morning:

> a silent singing (a vibration
over the trickling dawn–music of creek water
as earth tilts ripple and pool eastward)
awakes in air
stirred yet quiet, tense with shadow
stretched through the valley until the sun
rising crumbles the mountain rim in flame.

For joy of it, water sparkles,
fire pales, bridge planks and grass are warm.
Sun up to sun down, sun up to

Afternoon:

        let water weave on some snow slope
an umbrella of cloud, a screen of itself, for
itself, of rain. The sun licking
the stream splashes
scalding light into shade, invades
the under surface of bridge and leaf
and shrivels water at root source and stem.

Heat pants from the rocks while earth
embraced in the sun's tyranny
tilts downward, eastward, away, towards

Evening:

       heat lingers. Air is tepid.
Darkness comes so slowly even in these deep canyons.
But night falls and the water's own breath,
cool, rises now,
rises towards the mountain walls
bare to the hidden moon, white
with moonlight. Far moon, cold light, memory

moving across the mountain's face,
pantomiming dawn-to-twilight
journeys from twilight till dawn.

Winter Evening

In the mountains, it is said,
the deer are dying by hundreds.
We know nothing of that
in the suburbs.

           The cougar,
and death by being devoured,
the snow starving and shrouding
with one economical gesture
are ancestral myth. Our century
clings to the novel.
Coffee and novels.

With all the town's usual
stirrings muffled in snow,
the train whistles, only,
howl against death
over the plump white hills,
the billowing roofs—
howl like Lear in his heartbreak,
savage as a new myth.

Encounter in Buffalo

The country lies flat, expressionless as the face of a stranger.
Not one hillock shelters a buried bone. The city:
a scene thin as a theater backdrop, where no doors open,
no streets extend beyond the view from the corner.

Only the railroad embankment is high, shaggy with grass.
Only the freight, knuckling a red sun under its wheels,
drags familiar box-car shapes down long perspectives
of childhood meals and all crossings at sunset.

With a look deep as the continent, with the casual greeting
of those who will meet again, it bestrides the viaduct.
Its span is the span of trestles above mountain gorges,
its roar the echo of streams still wearing away stone.

The Whisperer

Where the sea runs a cobalt wedge under the coast bridges
and rhododendrons burn cool above concrete piers, an eddy of air
at the bridgehead will be I, as much I as
walks alone here between watered lawns at moonrise.

The eyes lie in daytime, that say these chairs, fields,
faces, are I, who am a strand of air raveling in the sound of leaves.
If the winds of the soul be unconsumed, I am lost,
left clinging at a bridgehead over sea water.

There is no reprieve in the touch of flowering trees.
Finger is sister to bark, both mute and solid, both
independent in death. Pity the poor soul, the public wind
imaged in language, proud to whirl papers down a littered street,
a draft at the door, whining for the bellows under your ribs.

The Rock of Levkas

You with the salt blue eyes
and a storm quivering under young ribs
sea-marked for coral:

You shrieked Fool! when she leapt,
her rigid feet taking the depth of the green
kelp-cloaked surge under the rocks.

The sea wallows in valleys deeper than these;
between remote continents it spins and knots
webs that will snare its rabbit in desert canyons.

Leave the seacoast, leave the river
hollowing its way to the sea.
Find your way into the pines and
higher than they grow, out upon glaciers—
you will not have escaped. Snow
will be whiter than foam between your lips,
tasteless, more quiet, and colder.

Remarks on Poetry and the Physical World

After reading *Ash Wednesday*
she looked once at the baked beans
and fled. Luncheonless, poor girl,
she observed a kind of poetic Lent—
and I had thought I liked poetry
better than she did.

I do. But to me its most endearing
quality is its unsuitableness;
and, conversely, the chief wonder in heaven
(whither I also am sometimes transported)
is the kind of baggage I bring with me.

Surely there is no more exquisite jointure
in the anatomy of life than that at which
poetry dovetails with the inevitable meal
and Mrs. B. sits murmuring of avocados.

Provincial

Mossy stones, the quilted legends
warming the villages like a sprigged comforter,
the dead like a smoke webbing the trees,
and all inviting dreaming:

These must be pleasant, but I never knew them,
have no acquaintance with bronze monuments,
have never spoken with a ghost on a bridge.
Our concrete piers are white and new in the water.

The dead are sparsely sown as yet.
The rain clouds rising above stumpland
form no apparitions. Thin wheat by the fir roots,
two potted geraniums on a stump
by the plank road receive the shower.

More beautiful than flowering moss
the naked rock rises,
chipped columnar by the liquid
blades of bright water.

Provincial II

The European made his appearance
wearing velvet and the jewels
of his inheritance
gravely, without unbecoming pride.

He courteously made it plain to her
the silk she wore was paper.
Dismayed, caught in the shower
of his disapproval, she bragged
in buckskin, which (he remarked)
was outdated fully one hundred years.
At last, cowering in a few rags
of homespun, she dried her tears with grass
and consoled herself with the large
plums of the provinces.

Note to a Neapolitan

On shipboard or in Naples
Miranda still walked on her island.
The palace floors ebbed from her private beaches.
Thought, that could not swim,
found no footing but on memory.

There is a green place in my mind
that paces my mind's conceptions.
The farthest-ranging of them
run with that colored shadow
under their sandals.
It gives them a foreign look
in brown places and gray places.

And Miranda emptied her shoes
of little pools of sand.

Suggested Miracle

The fishing boats lie on the spring flood,
one motor awakening over the water, and soon quieted.
Fishing looks an idle occupation,
idle as mine: gillnetting
at the confluence of two rivers
for fish of two colors.

My townspeople, my acquaintance, may I
lower you under this river
nose to nose with the salmon?
The silver and red fish of my catch
do not tempt you. Salmon would be a preferable food
if interviewed before eaten.

Drama

There are those who watch the papers for her name:
she passed here, was seen on the beach.
They think that Drama is, herself, an actress,
not the ever-present third in all rooms that hold two,
not the drowsy guest that every hostess finds
making a fifth at bridge, her head inert
upon the table edge, her hair
tangled among the cards. At dinner time the drone
of conversation is a lullaby
and smoke an opium cloud about her head.
But if a clumsy sleeve should brush her dress
so that she stirs,
silence bursts in the ears before the drone resumes.
Oh, sleep, sleep. We're all dead. Sleep, dear.
In the candlelight we watch her palpitant lids
and prowl about her on tiptoes,
fingers to lips. Oh hush, hush.

Carillon

In the morning, early, sitting
eating our loaves on weedgrown milestones
at the edge of the city, we hear the bells
swinging, challenging the attentive air.

The four-leaved pattern of a quarter hour
unfolds its conundrum; oh what
will the day bring? What, when the bells
ring evening, will we remember?
Of hours and quarter hours, which
will be honey-tongued? Which echo
in the stroke of all hours forever?

At twilight the sphinx in the bell tower
answers her riddle, ringing: Remember?
Remember wondering: oh what will the day bring?

They Are Excited

about

"ideas which they
apprehend but do
not comprehend."

Fog too settles
close over all
cabbage blue rain-

water patches
pondwater blue
cabbage patches

and up the hills.
On top—

six geese, distinct
as Chinese brushwork,
stretch their wings

in sunlight on
a misty field.

The Spring

The water whispers in a quick
flow out from under a boulder
to moisten the thick-standing mint.

It fills the pond, goes down over
the spillway and under the road.
It fills another small pond, then

falls quickly away between tall
cottonwoods, a mere trickle still,
to find its fate in the river.

Nameless, it has two little ponds
to its credit, like a poet
with two small collections of verse.

For this I celebrate it.

Two Visits

1. E. P.: Martinsbrunn, 1961

It is an old old shaman
with his hair long, his face
laid bare to the bone.

The masks have all slipped off
except a death–mask stark
as marble; his hands are warm.

The eyes, alive, look sharply
from the skull but distantly as
if from the moon's deadlands

where he has been, possessed
ghosts, and they him: his jaws
unhinged by death will sing.

2. E. P.: Sant'Ambrogio, 1964

Names make news, and today the name
is the Possum's, the nickname audible
even in the drumroll from overseas.

Drums and trumpets, and all that folly—
or so it seems here on the silent hill,
climbing the wet stones of the *salita*.

The firm old feet, soft-shod, go up before me
as quietly as rain falls on the olive leaves,
the eyes and the sea both distant and still
as if we were standing high, high on Parnassus.

Fable of the Ant and the Word

Ink-black, but moving independently
across the black and white parquet of print,
the ant cancels the author out. The page,
translated to itself, bears hair-like legs
disturbing the fine hairs of its fiber.
These are the feet of summer, pillaging meaning,
destroying Alexandria. Sunlight is silence
laying waste all languages, until, thinly,
the fictional dialogue begins again:
the page goes on telling another story.

Anadyomene

This is confusion of sea mist,
a white clot of it, bred of uncertain weather.

A cloud, that has no skeleton,
skin, lips, or any defined
outline, could not
moving feel more wonder,
moving without volition
towards the bare mountain.

See where the sunlit headland
changes! Light-dazzle on rock fades
and shadow softens. Cliffs, rising,
widen in encircling vapor—
cloudself, a nothingness which
touching the warm stone
distils radiance.

Far down, the sea,
loud on the rocks.

Inheritance

I have no inheritance in
the only sense you know—one teaspoon
out of a Virginian dozen
that twinkled after Boone's
bold star into Kentucky.
Spoon clink fell to axe-chink
falling along the Ohio. Those women
made their beds, God bless them,
in the wandering, dreamed, hoped-for
Hesperides, their graves
in permanent places.

And, dying, left no inheritance?
I call to witness those women,
(Mary Marshall, Mary Noel—
did they leave me only their names?—
Polly Connor, Susan Carroll)
whose daughters had a woman's value.
My own pride is theirs
descended through that willful girl
proudest of all, who turned
twenty on her death-bed—

And, dying, left me neither pride
of place, nor pride of blood,
but memory of the pride of
her love, and a night ride,
a thing easy to carry, the right
thing to be found dead in:
armor stronger than silver
against time and men and women.

Height Is the Distance Down

What's geography? What difference what mountain
it is? In the intimacy of this altitude
its discolored snowfields overhang half the world.

On a knife rim edge-up into whirlpools of sky,
feet are no anchor. Gravity sucks at the mind
spinning the blood-weighted body head downward.

The mountain that had become a known profile
on the day's horizon is a gesture of earth
swinging us above falling spaces, above
a map of the world. Disturber of the unseen,
provoker of the gusts in which we bend
struggling against destruction gaping eastward.
The wind fails. The breath held. The illusion of death.
The resisting shoulder unopposed lurches
west in innocent still air, as steep, as deep.

Persephone

I lived like a mole. There were
subterranean flat stone stairways
to columns supporting the earth and its
daffodils. Or shall we say, to the façade
of the hiding place of earth's treasure?

From there in any direction
one walked endlessly upon short grass tufts
stiff as cactus in the aridity of cold.
The lake wharves were icebound;
the wind, unending, circling the earth's interior,
brought no news.
                    Homesickness here
is for the raw working and scars of the surface:
furrows, quarries, split wood . . .
Thirst drawing the throat is for warm blood,
speech with the living. And hunger—to which
(the long table, the tentative offering
of fruit from lost orchards)
                        surrender is death.

How many times it is said to the living,
Conquer hunger! If you
want to go back, up, up where the sun falls
warm on flowering rock and make garlands again.

Midnight

Now the dead lend us
peace for the dark hours.

At midnight the never-to-awaken
sleep lightly; yet those who lay
in love at death-fall have quiet to lend.

Only the murdered must walk.
The murderer clutches at sleep
as at scant covers; wakes chilled.

Come now,
comes now death-lent oblivion. I love
her who died unknown to me.
I adjust my bones to the composure
of hers.
Peace fall on my exile
from hers.

The Field

Sweep the mind
                    clean
like a field of dry stubble
when the constellations
of daisies have been mown.

Let it be lit by stars
rooted outside the seasons . . .

To the flesh of the field
alive with worm and seed
tomorrow is in the night wind;
while drought or rain
spirals towards earth
mortal stirrings demand
horoscopes of the stars.

Weather is all.

Crossroads

Rotting in the wet gray air
the railroad depot stands deserted under
still green trees. In the fields
cold begins an end.

There were other too-long-postponed departures.
They left, finally, because of well water
gone rank, the smell of fungus, the chill
of rain in chimneys.

The spot is abandoned even in memory.
They knew, locking doors upon empty houses,
to leave without regret is to lose
title to one home forever.

Later: Four Fragments

1.
Tired we watch
a low sun shaping
hillock and hollow
in what were
noon's flat meadows.

2.
Don't let them tell you
it will all come right
in the end. It won't.
It won't. It won't. Never.
Death is always the end.

3.
Once the sea flowed before us
as far as the Four Quarters,
to ten thousand unknown ports.
See how it narrows
to a ribbon track behind.

4.
The dams have drowned
the rapids and white water
curls in memory with eyes
and voices that come clear
only between sleeping and waking.

Three Translations from the Greek

1. Ball Game

Golden haired Love
calls me (tossing
me his bright ball)

to come play at
catch with a young
thing in red sandals.

But she, being off
prosperous Lesbos,
finds fault with my

gray hairs: she hangs
around open-mouthed
after another man.

(*after* Anacreon)

2. Terpander

This poet died
singing in the
village square;

he was not hit
by an arrow,
not by a sword.

Death always has
some excuse: he
choked on a fig.

(*after* Tryphon)

3. Inscription

I was not: I became.
I was: and I am not.
And that is all. If anyone
says otherwise, he lies.
I shall not be.

(*from the* Anthology)

Static

I wanted to hear
Sappho's laughter
and the speech of
her stringed shell.

What I heard was
whiskered mumble-
ment of grammarians:

Greek pterodactyls
and Victorian dodos.

Chronos

Days equal
years, years
days: the scales

of the easy-
does–it old
calculator

(as they tried
to tell Elec-
tra) hold level.

Late Roman

I shall be
an historic
figure also,
Mr. Achilles.

One digit in
one of Gibbon's
many footnotes
will denote ME!

Ceremony

The cups were polished
coconut shells cut
lengthwise; they were

never placed upon
the floor itself,
but on bark cloth

laid before priest
or server; never
where one might by

stepping over
desecrate them.
The ceremony

being ended they
were placed in nets
hanging from rafters,

for they were sacred
like the drink they
held
        or like the god.

I like to think of these cups,
mornings, picking up
the beer cans on the lawn.

Letter from Byzantium

If you aren't Green, the Greens
will beat you up; if you aren't Blue,
the Blues will smash your shop.
The Emperor won't put a stop
to it. He belongs to the Greens.

If you don't care who wins, it means
you don't care, whoever kills
you: no doubt they both will.

Men have died bloodily in the past.
It has to happen, Priam said, so that
great poets may have stories to tell.

In the year One Nine Nine Two
a scholarly dissertation on Green and Blue
will be written, not published.
Only the author will care then what the row
was about and nobody will care more
for chariot racing than I do now.

Adversity and the Generations

Mules and mulish children,
the obstinacy of boulders
embedded in arable soil,
the extreme tenaciousness
of roots in the wrong places
and intractable weather
were, we suppose, the scourges
of Cain also, toiling before
Eden's east threshold.

But we were not content.
Full of ambition, with capacity
for increased exasperation,
we devise a pancake machine.
The pancake batter, as always,
creating a delicate situation,
the electrically animated parts
miscalculate exactly.

Thistles and thorns were nothing
to this dogged inaccurate motion
producing lunch-counter chaos.
Cain was bitter, but his seed
suffer hysteria.

Eternal She

Outside the brick tomb that protects
not Placidia's dust but certain mosaics
the art lover may sniff warm clover.

A clarion cackle derides Roman
lawgiver and barbaric invader:

Tut tut tut! Alaric, Justin-
ian was it or Theodoric
got uppity? What of it? Look look
look at it! I did it! Look at it!

There is a new egg in Ravenna.

To a Lie-Adept

In a shadowed corner
she rolled another's sorrow
under her tongue like a sweet caramel.
Truth became obscene in her mouth.

From one like her I may learn finally
to come back to you in all humbleness,
knowing the shameful uses of truth,
desiring to be taught the craft of liars
and how to prepare, as you do, fiction suitable
for a disordered appetite.

Nor shall I dispense
occasional cinnamon drops.
Rather, I will lie as you do,
urging whole succulent messes, whole platterfuls,
upon the gluttonous guest.

Prometheus Loved Us

I walk in a twilight half-drawn
along the edge of the town,
walk with rain on my coatsleeves,
drops clinging upon the prongs of the wool.
Should I record anything?

Runnel of rain at the curb will
drop down to the river. Vacant lots
spill grass on the sidewalk
and I walk nowhere in particular.
Nothing.

Except that the merest match-wing
of fire pricks through the rain
and the street is stung to life.
Heart leaps, like a fish striking.

Fawn

Out of a high meadow where flowers
bloom above cloud, come down;
pursue me with reasons for smiling without malice.

Bring mimic pride like that of the seedling fir,
surprise in the perfect leg-stems
and queries unstirred by recognition or fear
pooled in the deep eyes.

Come down by regions where rocks
lift through the hot haze of pain;
down landscapes darkened, crossed
by the rift of death-shock; place print
of a neat hoof on trampled ground
where not one leaf or root
remains unbitten; but come down
always, accompany me to the morass
of the decaying mind. There
we'll share one rotted stump between us.

In Praise of Potted Plants

With the wet snow that falls
before the beginning of spring,
the dark flowers put forth buds
in hearts which expect nothing.

Bring only flowers
into the invalid's chamber.
Let no squirrel intrude
and although a marmot
raise unanswerable questions
he does so without dignity.
He nibbles (God help him!)
at his tragedy.

Bring humorless flowers
to complement those we imagine
dark in the heart. Surround us
with the grave perfume of plants.

The Pump

In the painted quiet
of snow ridges
above peacock rivers
and blond grass scant
over ledges of rock

a pump is quietly
companionable, beating
under the hollow ribs
of untenanted canyons,

unseen, working
to what purpose?

The little slingshot
of sound challenges
an invulnerable silence.

Noon Hour

The red-hatted mill
owners are eating
pears; their hunting
rifles trail dwarf
shadows through pine,
swinging in step;

longtailed puppies
yipping scamper
around slow boots.

The mill crew is one
merry old man wearing
a red rag on his hat:
a bearded Noah perched
on ark-lumber.

The stag sighted
at midmorning
was safe at noon.

Real Estate

In late May the grasses
are so tall their plumy
waving tops conceal
a sign saying FOR SALE

by Whitfield Bros. The fields
that lately pastured mules
have now become "homesites"
with "riverviews" but still

are rich in clover, lupine,
vetch—rank flowering weeds
fragrant and peaceful, rustling
above wires laid underground.

Picture Window

The gulls by day, the moon by night
pass and repass the window, weaving time;
opposite, the clock ticks; I move between.
The mailbox watches by the roadside.

The window trembles in its frame
and hums, tuned by the thundering of jets
concealed in cloud. On the river a tugboat
seems motionless with its slow load.

Rain spatters on the glass and smears
the view; sun drenches the drawn curtains.
I wait and watch. A rabbit in the rosebed
completes a corner of the afternoon.

The Solitary

The lone drake, upended,
nibbles the pond bottom,
red legs paddling the air.

He sleeps on the rock wall
by the spillway, balanced
on one foot, head hidden.

In the shadowed shallows
under sycamore boughs
the encircling ripples

have one center: himself.
Intruders, including
mallards of his own race,

beautiful strangers, drive
him to frenzied attack,
quacking, snapping, churning

the pond. When they have gone
bright wavelets unbroken
to the rim spread round him.

Probably Nobody

Twenty crows
(charred paper)
litter the
frosted ground.

Small yellow
apples gleam
nakedly through
bare twigs.

Who'll buy red
rose haws white
snowberries

or a crane
mirrored in
slough water?

Soft Chains

Soft chains are most
difficult to break:
affection, ease.

The spirit, wide-eyed,
limp-muscled, nestles
on its side
         and waits

Now

I never wanted to kill
myself, never wanted
to die; but now, looking
ahead, thinking of thought
some day going awry
and trickling to a stop,
leaving a smelly shell
high on a dry beach

I think—
            almost
I think—
            but
No. Not yet.

VII

The Pleiades

They are heard as a choir of seven
shining voices; they descend
like a flock of wild swans to the water.

The white wing plumage folds;
they float on the lake—seven
stars reflected among the reeds.

Tonight, the Seven Little Sisters,
daughters of the Moon, will come down
to bathe or wash their summer dresses.

They wear costumes of the seven
rainbow colors, they wear feather
mantles they can lift in sea winds

raised by their singing, and so rise
flying, soaring, until they fade
as the moon dawns; their voices dwindle

and die out in the North Woods, over
Australian bush, from Spartan
dancing grounds and African beaches.

They have returned to the sky
for the last time, and even
Electra's weeping over Troy is stilled.

What girl or star sings now
like a swan on the Yellow River?

A Picture of the Moon

Photography has laid a waste
of sand over the last outpost.
Mythology is displaced.

No longer will Chinese magicians
swinging in space on silken belts
alight upon the lunar coast

and toast Heng O in elixir.
Her dancers in their rainbow silks
are, with the peach trees, lost.

The snowy Tiger of the West—
oh, where is he? And where
the Cassia Tree? the Toad of Time?
All now are lunar dust.

Lai

Nothing availed then in the starless darkness with the sea giving a gray
    light.
Nothing availed then either by sea or by land
for the boats were filled with a shallow and unlit water, their sails riven.
But her hands spread upon the bolt of the door refused to believe
and the waves spoke for her since she had no voice.

I said, striving with her, "He is long since dead.
I have seen the queens who ride fast along dark roads
bearing death upon their lips and love upon the palms of their hands.
I know they now have left the mired ways and the channelled meadows.
Where blue roads echo under the stripped high-singing trees, tower-ward
    they bear him.
In the yellow tideland shallow water laps unheard."

But she shook her head and the waves spoke for her as they do still,
sighing a furtive song in the spread foam
while the troubled stones of the beach turn in my heart.

Ondine

At supper time an ondine's narrow feet
made dark tracks on the hearth.
Like the heart of a yellow fruit was the fire's heat,
but they rubbed together quite blue with the cold.
The sandy hem of her skirt dripped on the floor.
She sat there with a silvered cedar knot
for a low stool; and I sat opposite,
my lips and eyelids hot
in the heat of the fire. Piling on dry bark,
seeing that no steam went up from her dark dress,
I felt uneasiness
as though firm sand had shifted under my feet
in the wash of a wave.

I brought her soup from the stove and she would not eat,
but sat there crying her cold tears,
her blue lips quivering with cold and grief.
She blamed me for a thief,
saying that I had burned a piece of wood
the tide washed up. And I said, No,
the tide had washed it out again; and even so,
a piece of sodden wood was not so rare
as polished agate stones or ambergris.

She stood and wrung her hair
so that the water made a sudden splash
on the round rug by the door. I saw her go
across the little footbridge to the beach.
After, I threw the knot on the hot coals.
It fell apart and burned with a white flash,
a crackling roar in the chimney and dark smoke.

I beat it out with a poker
in the soft ash.

Now I am frightened on the shore at night,
and all the phosphorescent swells that rise
come towards me with the threat of her dark eyes
with a cold firelight in them;
and crooked driftwood writhes
in dry sand when I pass.

Should she return and bring her sisters with her,
the withdrawing tide
would leave a long pool in my bed.
There would be nothing more of me this side
the melting foamline of the latest wave.

Wine Ship

A mast askew in the surf,
wood of another climate
bedded forever in half-liquid sand.

The sharp-eared foreigner
struggling out of the sea-wrack
felt his flesh wither in the cold winds of this coast.

Here were no myrtle groves,
no familiar shrines,
only the splintered casks and the sweet wines
spilt in the sea.

Here were no grapes,
but bitter berries grew in the marsh.

Here was no moss,
but sea worn logs and the harsh
grass on the dune top.

In this forlorn meeting of sea and land
mirth is lost over the stormy water
and the sand
lies suddenly cold under the hand.

From this shore an exile learns
to keep where a fire burns,
but there is no disguise
in small hand or white throat
when still by night a disturbing rhythm returns
from groves forgotten.

When the long eyelids are lifted
suddenly, outlandish lights appear
in the woman's eyes: we think we hear
the tap of hidden hooves
somewhere in our closed corridors.

Cassandra

Write of her if you will, but never try
to speak as though in her person, "I, Cassandra—"
Speak of her as the least of the Trojan
women might have spoken
after they learned that captives do not die,
but suffer inconveniences of exile.

If we knew how the world looked, turning
into the shadow, if any woman stood
as she did by Apollo's shoulder
and caught the smell of burning
even before night closed upon the towers—
she would have little care for what was said
in a city seven times buried.
Her mind would be a cauldron. She would have
no thought for the dead.

Odysseus Speaking
(from the *Odyssey*, opening of Book IX)

I am Odysseus, the son of Laertes: men everywhere
tell stories of me, until news of my tricks must,
I think, have reached heaven. Ithaca is my home,
an island of clear skies and a wooded windswept
hill, Mount Neriton—an island that lies
close to its neighbor islands of Samë, Doulíchion
and wooded Zacynthos, yet more to seaward, turned
to the west while they face dawn and sunrise.
It is a hard land, a breeder of men; and I know
no sweeter sight than a man's own country;
the goddess Calypso held me in her rock-walled
cave, wishing to marry me; Circe, the sorceress,
kept me in her high halls, wishing to marry me;
but neither of them could ever persuade my heart,
because this is true: his own country, his own
kindred are what any man loves most, though you find him
settled among foreigners in some richer home.

Fable from the Cayoosh Country

As we lay at the lake edge, feet pointing northwest,
our thought pushed forward into the margins of silence.
There would be the crying of creeks, birds,
and animal young, but verbal silence.
A region crowded with nameless mountains.

Thorn branches sheltered the beach,
graying the arrested twilight.
Indians passed at our feet,
averted profiles moving against the clear lake,
against the boundaries of an inarticulate world.

We slept, and our minds crawled with words.
Footloose words ran about in our dreams.

I went, a missionary, into the mountains,
taking the grammars of all languages.
I preached the blessing of the noun and verb,
but all was lost in the furred ear of the bear,
in the expressive ear of the young doe.
What the doe said with her ear, I understood.
What I said, she obviously did not.

Despairing, I flung my textbooks into a rocky pool,
and the stream turned through the volumes, speaking clearly.

"Where my monologue runs, there was once the debate of the beasts.
The burrows bubbled with words, conversation
issued from the mouths of caves.
Where there was speech there is now only my voice.
Had the mountain goat need of his eloquence
to make of his native rocks a rostrum?

Did the beaver's young learn industrious ways of a proverb?
The humming bird was a fiction. What legend could please her?

"The blade of this tool, useless for digging, chopping,
shearing, they used against each other with such zeal
they all but accomplished their own extermination.
Then—they abandoned speech!
They retained cries expressive of emotion,
as rage, or love. That was all.
That was eons ago.
Consider this thing," said the stream, in six languages.
"They have never seen any cause to repent their decision."

I dreamed then, of a tide in the lake.
It rose over us where we slept
and flooded southward into the settled country.
My consternation was that of a poet, whose love
if not his living was gravely endangered.

I awoke, and the lake was in place.
Perhaps that was a pity. A purification . . . ?
Perhaps if one rose now and bathed in the water?

Blood Ritual

Pestilence, violence, distress attendant
on the sharpening seasons
are part of us and our incessant commotion.
The tree stems offer no remonstrance.
Does she who stood between them
wait underground for peace again
as though the lilac should not bloom while hunger lasted?
Or is our passion acceptable as rain?

The pulp that swells the green skin of the grape
is hard in its unripeness, indicating
a time before the violet eyes trembled
and the flesh knew its hunter.
The frozen mountain, falling as the road falls
behind the scarlet leaf-burn of this season
refers to it and to the curtains of quiet.
She will have a loveless peace then.

Adoring her in all her manifestations,
I think how Apollo without his sacrifice
has lost his godhead. The flower will not sing on its stem,
nor the fruit utter a cry as it falls.
Why should not the flesh of the innocent
while it endures, smoke on her altars?

Lethe

Above the brink
of that lamentable river I shall lean,
hesitant, unwilling to drink,
as I remember there for the last time.

Will a few drops on the tongue,
like a whirling flood submerge cities,
like a sea, grind pillars to sand?
Will it wash the color from the lips and the eyes
beloved? It were a thousand pities
thus to dissolve
the delicate sculpture of a lifted hand,
to fade the dye
of the world's color, to quench forever
the fires of earth in this river.

The living will forget
more quickly than I,
dead, lingering with lips unwet
above Lethe.

This book was designed by John Laursen during the summer of 1979. 700 clothbound copies, on natural Sonata vellum, were produced in the first printing, of which 100 had a leather spine and were numbered and signed by the poet. 2000 softbound copies on Warren's Olde Style have been produced in the second printing, October 1981. The typography, using Bembo type and Sistina Titling, is by Irish Setter. The labyrinth design is from a woodcut by Anita Bigelow.

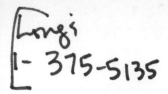

Long's

1- 375-5135

375-6707 home